TWISTED TUNES

PETER QUIGLEY

ACKNOWLEDGEMENTS

This book would not have been possible without the support of my family. My mother and father, who will unfortunately not be able to ever see this book in person, have supported me for years and years in so many ways. I will be forever grateful and wish I could pay them back for everything they have done for me, but I know I can't and never will. My kids and especially my wife who has gone through so much and has ALWAYS been there for me no matter how crazy, weird, silly, irresponsible, forgetful, selfish (and the list goes on!) I have been. Thank you, family! I love you all! And remember... keep smiling!

DEDICATION

Dedicated to my loving parents, Hugh and Elizabeth.

Where it all began.

TABLE OF CONTENTS

IT'S HOW TWINS ARE BORN

To the tune of "Riders On The Storm" by The Doors.

It's how twins are born
It's how twins are born

Into this house they're born
Into this world they're thrown
It's two ova and two sperm
Two children at full term

It's how twins are born

Use no pill or use no foam
And they'll be squirming toward their home
Two kids were born today
Let the parents pray

You know two is twice the task
Next time you'll have to ask
"Pill or use the foam?"

Girl, you need a helping hand?
Girl, you need a helping hand?
Wish you had four hands?
Sounds like a good plan
They'll soon be in Depends
Our job is done by then
Need a helping hand?

It's how twins are born
It's how twins are born

Into this house they're born
Into this world they're thrown
It's two ova and two sperm
Two children at full term

It's how twins are born

It's how twins are born
It's how twins are born
It's how twins are born
It's how twins are born

SALISBURY MEAL

To the tune of "Solsbury Hill" by Peter Gabriel.

Heating up a Salisbury meal
I turned on the oven light
It was warming, broke the seal
A long day, I eat at night

Buzzer rings, done with pre-heat
Put it in, what time to set?
Drinking, waiting soon to eat
20 minutes, do not fret

I do not believe it has nutrition
Will it cause heartburn, indigestion?
My heart going, "No, no, no"
"Salt," it said
"Fatty things will drive the stake right home"

What other stuff they put in here?
It does not look like the picture
Tastes better with lager beer
Whether a glass or pitcher

So hungry I'll eat the tray
Not the best, it fills my gut
Think I'll live another day
Or I'll face a surgeon's cut

I should have had a salad greenery
Not this stuff out of the machinery
My heart going "No, no, no!"
"Hey," it said
"Fatty things will drive the stake right home"
Yeah, right home!

Chicken machine separate
Beef, water, corn, and soy protein
Onion was dehydrated
Definitely not fat-free

Hit the spot, I did survive
Maybe I should have had the fish
Feel funny, am I alive?
Or is this the devil's wish?

Should've kept it right on the store shelf
Walk by the freezer door and save yourself
My heart going "No! No! No!"
"Hey!" it said
"All that crap just drove that stake right home!"

I'M A DECEIVER

To the tune of "I'm A Believer" by The Monkees.

I thought that I could get by with skillful play
Win by learning all tricks of the trade
It was working for me
At least so it seemed
'Til one day I realized all my dreams

Have a poker face, cuz I'm a deceiver
You can't read what is on my mind
A full house
I'm a deceiver, you thought I had 3-of-a-kind

I thought that I could do the president thing
People saw right through my fake façade
So, I just stopped tryin'
It was way too hard
Quit political game, took up cards

Have a poker face, cuz I'm a deceiver
You can't read what is on my mind
A full house
I'm a deceiver, you thought I had 3-of-a-kind

Oh, deceiver
Oh, it was working for me
At least so it seemed
'Til one day I realized all my dreams

Have a poker face, cuz I'm a deceiver
You can't read what is on my mind
A full house
I'm a deceiver, you thought I had 3-of-a-kind

Yes, a poker face now I'm a deceiver
You can't read what is on my mind
Said I'm a deceiver
Yeah, yeah, yeah, yeah, yeah, yeah
"(I'm a deceiver)"
Said I'm a deceiver,
"Yeah (I'm a deceiver)
I said I'm a deceiver
Yeah (I'm a deceiver)

SHUTDOWN

To the tune of "Blackout" by Scorpions.

I realize something's amiss
As the earth was touched by Satan's kiss
It spread quickly to my home space
Lost my smell and I lost my taste

I'm in quarantine
with COVID-19

I do puzzles for a fix
I start binge watching shows on Netflix
I change the way I do school
Everything now has different rules

I'm wearing a mask
To do every task

Shut down
I'm really in a shutdown
Shut down
I'm really in a shutdown
Shut down
I'm really in a shutdown
Shut down
I'm really in a shutdown

There's no commute, I work from home
Really strange, I feel so alone
Will this stop, or is there more?
I have to get to the grocery store

I'm in quarantine
with COVID-19

Shut down
I'm really in a shutdown
Shut down
I'm really in a shutdown
Shut down
I'm really in a shutdown
Shut down
I'm really in a shutdown
I'm really in a shutdown, baby

I'm in quarantine
with COVID-19

Shut down
I'm really in a shutdown
Shut down
I'm really in a shutdown
Shut down
I'm really in a shutdown
Shut down
I'm really in a shutdown

Shutdown
Shutdown
Shutdown

RUBBER DUCKY

To the tune of "You Got Lucky" by Tom Petty.

I'm Ernie with a striped shirt
I'm Ernie with a tub full of suds
I was playing with dirt
I need someone to help with the crud

Toy
Fave toy
I remembered
I need a bath tonight
I need a bath tonight
Rubber ducky, Bert
Rubber ducky, Bert
And the soap, too

I just need my squeaky friend
To help me scrub and sing a song
Till Sesame Street's end
All the TV kids can sing along

My toy
Fave toy
I remembered
I need a bath tonight
I need a bath tonight
Rubber ducky, Bert
Rubber ducky, Bert
And the soap, too

Fave toy
My toy
I remembered
I need a bath tonight
I need a bath tonight
Rubber ducky, Bert
Rubber ducky, Bert
And the soap, too

PASS THE GLUE

To the tune of "Love Me Do" by The Beatles.

I, I need glue
I do crafts like you
My bottle is through

So please
Pass the glue
Whoa, I need glue

I, I need glue
I fix things like you
My bottle is through

So please
Pass the glue
Whoa, I need glue

Some at the store, gorilla glue
Some at the store, aisle G2

I, I need glue
This one piece is two
My bottle is through

So please
Pass the glue
Whoa, I need glue

I, I need glue
Yes, that sticky goo
My bottle is through

So please
Pass the glue
Whoa, pass the glue

Yeah, pass the glue
Whoa-oh, pass the glue

CIRCUMCISION

To the tune of "Double Vision" by Foreigner.

I was just a baby, way before a teen
Between birth and the time I had to ween
Parents had a third son, they didn't want to wait
Want it to be normal when I use it straight

Anesthetize before circumcision
No pain here for my circumcision
Ooh, it was done in a snap
Removal of the wrap
My circumcision was the best for me

It was just done, and I had no choice
I was put under, didn't hear the doctor's voice
When it was done, assistants all began their clapping
Doctor with a smile said, "That's Reynolds wrapping!"

Anesthetize before circumcision
No pain here for my circumcision
Ooh, it was done in a snap
Removal of the wrap
My circumcision always seemed to be a need for me
Need for me, yeah
Ooh, circumcision, I need a circumcision
They took it off of my head, takin' it off of my head
I got my circumcision, sawing circum circum
Oh, got my circumcision (oh, circumcision) yeah
Oh, I've got a circumcision

EAT BRAN

To the tune of "Roxanne" by The Police.

Eat bran
You can't seem to move that poop tonight
No use for TP
You don't have to flush your toilet on this night

Eat bran
You don't have to wear Depends tonight
No three states of matter
You haven't sat for so long and that's not right

Eat bran
You can't seem to move that poop tonight
Eat bran
You can't seem to move that poop tonight

Eat bran (moving poop tonight)
Eat bran (moving poop tonight)
Eat bran (moving poop tonight)
Eat bran (moving poop tonight)
Eat bran (moving poop tonight)

Eat bran
You can't seem to move that poop tonight
Eat bran
You can't seem to move that poop tonight

Eat bran (you can't seem to move that poop tonight)
Eat bran (moving poop tonight)
Eat bran (moving poop tonight)
Eat bran (moving poop tonight)
Eat bran (moving poop tonight)
Eat bran (moving poop tonight)
Eat bran (moving poop tonight)
Eat bran (moving poop tonight)
Eat bran (moving poop tonight)
Eat bran (moving poop tonight)
Eat bran (you can't seem to move that poop tonight)
Eat bran (moving poop tonight)
Eat bran (you can't seem to move that poop tonight)
Eat bran (moving poop tonight)
Eat bran (moving poop tonight)

You hated constipation
You're part of bloating nation
An oat bran breakfast, and now you feel
You won't have to wait another day
High fiber is the new rule
A softer, flowing new stool
Do it once, and you'll do it again
It's a new way

BLEEDING BADLY

To the tune of "Love Her Madly" by The Doors.

You are bleeding badly
Need compression sadly
Need to elevate
What did doctors say?

You are bleeding badly
You don't look good, Maddie
Much blood on her face
Need to clean up before walkin' out the door
Before slipping on the bloody floor

Need to elevate
What did doctors say?
Need to clean up before walkin' out the door

All your blood
All your blood
All your blood
All your blood
All your blood is gone
Leaving before too long
It was done so clean
Seven stitches seam
Need a note for work

Yeah, you were bleeding
Got to clean up before walkin' out the door

All your blood
All your blood
All your blood
Yeah, all your blood is gone
Leaving before too long
It was done so clean
Seven stitches seam
Need a note for work

You are bleeding badly
You are bleeding badly
You are bleeding badly

GAMBLIN' MAN

To the tune of "Ramblin' Man" by The Allman Brothers Band.

Lord, I was born a gamblin' man
Start with dice a-rollin', and five cards in my hand
And when the night is over
Winnings are in my hands
I have become a gamblin' man

Well, my father would play with change in the basement
He'd come home at 3 AM with less or more
And I would think to myself that I could be like him
But I'd win 5 or 10 times more

Lord, I was born a gamblin' man
Start with dice a-rollin', and five cards in my hand
And when the night is over
Winnings are in my hands
I have become a gamblin' man

Alright
We're on our way to New Jersey this morning
Leaving out of Reading to A.C
They're always growing jackpots in the casinos
Lord, hitting one would be the end of me

Lord, I was born a gamblin' man
Start with dice a-rollin', and five cards in my hand
And when the night is over
Winnings are in my hands
I have become a gamblin' man

Lord, I was born a gamblin' man
Lord, I was born a gamblin' man
Lord, I was born a gamblin' man
Lord, I was born a gamblin' man

WELCOME TO THE BIRD NEST

To the tune of "Welcome To The Jungle" by Guns N' Roses.

Welcome to the Bird Nest, we've won 14 games
We know how to kick some ass and always taking names
We are the Philly team from the division in the East
Now we're off to play that team that's also from the East
In the Bird Nest, welcome to the Bird Nest
Bring the Pats down to their sha na na na na na na knees, knees!
Let's, let's watch Brady bleed

Welcome to the Bird Nest, we took it game by game
Our fans were always right behind us if Wentz could not play
But you're so very determined, so hard to defeat
You can taste the playoffs, but you won't get there for free
In the Bird Nest, welcome to the Bird Nest

Wear my my my my Eagles green
I want to hear you scream!

Welcome to the Bird Nest, we got Foles now everyday
You learn to play like an animal in the Bird Nest where we play

If you got a hunger for that trophy, we'll take it eventually
You can have anything you want just not the Lombardi!
In the Bird Nest, Welcome to the Bird Nest
Bring Brady to his sha na na na na na na knees, knees!
We're going to watch him plead!

Hey that catch was never, ever touching the ground
First down! First down! First down! Yaaaaay!

You know where you are?
You're in the Bird Nest, Brady
You're gonna die!

In the Bird Nest, welcome to the Bird Nest
Bring the Pats down to their sha na na na na na na knees, knees
In the Bird Nest, welcome to the Bird Nest
Wear my my my my Eagles green
Bird Nest, welcome to the Bird Nest
Brings the Pats down to their sha na na na na na na knees, knees!
Down in the Bird Nest, welcome to the Bird Nest
Watch them bring it to you
They're going to take you down. HA!!

RUN TO MY PILLS

To the tune of "Run To The Hills" by Iron Maiden.

My name is called, doctor sees me
To rid my pain and misery
I've tried yoga and CBD
Prescription pills is what I need

I've fought the pain, I fought it well
Can not no more, I live in hell
Will my Cigna plan cover me?
Oh, will I ever be pain free?

Smoking the weed, it leaves a bad taste
I cannot take it no more
Split them, crush them, or taking them
whole
Before I writhe on the floor
Get in my system, and run through my veins
Starting to work, I feel normal again

Run to my pills
Take four or five
Run to my pills
Take four or five

Run for refills, no time to waste
Needing to kill all the pain
Working the whole day and working all night
I'm feeling like myself again
There's no addiction, I do what I'm told
I'm popping pills young and I'll pop when I'm
old

Run to my pills
Take four or five
Run to my pills
Take four or five

Run to my pills
Take four or five
Run to my pills
Take four or five

Run to my pills
Take four or five
Run to my pills
Take four or five

LOSIN' ALL MY HAIR

To the tune of "Livin' on a Prayer" by Bon Jovi.

My genes from my dad really suck
I'm folically weak
Try to keep it in, it's tough, so tough
Bosley couldn't help me at all
Working with that guy would take all my pay
That's bull——— that's bull———

I say I've got to hold on to what I've got
It doesn't make a difference if I brush it or
not
Unlike my brother
Soon to be gone, you'll see
I don't have a lot

Whoa, I'm halfway there
Whoa, oh losin' all my hair
Don't need a comb or bottle of Nair
Whoa, oh losin' all my hair

I've only got a few hair strands
A strong gust of wind will blow them in my
hands
So tough, it's tough
My wife says, "Shave it away"
She just might be right
But I whisper, "Maybe someday"
"Someday"

I've got to hold on to what I've got
It doesn't make a difference if I brush it or not
Unlike my brother
Soon to be gone you'll see
I don't have a lot

Whoa, I'm halfway there
Whoa, oh losin' all my hair
Don't need a comb or bottle of Nair
Whoa, oh losin' all my hair

Losin' all my hair

Oh, it's going to fall out, ready or not
Cream and a razor is what I just bought

Whoa, I'm halfway there
Whoa, oh losin' all my hair
Don't need a comb or bottle of Nair
Whoa, oh losin' all my hair

Whoa, I'm halfway there
Whoa, oh losin' all my hair
Don't need a comb or bottle of Nair
Whoa, oh losin' all my hair

Whoa, I'm halfway there
Whoa, oh losin' all my hair
Don't need a comb or bottle of Nair
Whoa, oh losin' all my hair

I GOT IT CHEAPER

To the tune of "(Don't Fear) The Reaper" by Blue Öyster Cult.

Monday trash truck comes
Grab, before they're gone
Sundays, I found it cheaper
Whether in the wind or sun, or the rain
"New" stuff cannot be far

Deckboards, baby (I got it cheaper)
Hey, look! Ceiling fan! (I got it cheaper)
There's no reason to buy (I got it cheaper)
Baby, pack your van

La la la la la
La la la la la

Bonus points are done
Used them, now they're gone
Mr. Pick and Mrs. Spot
Are together in this trash journey (Mr. Pick
and Mrs. Spot)
40,000 men and women everyday (like Mr.
Pick and Mrs. Spot)
40,000 men and women everyday (Redefine
flipping things)
Another 40,000 joining everyday (New stuff
cannot be far)

Deckboards, baby (I got it cheaper)
Hey, look! Ceiling fan! (I got it cheaper)
There's no reason to buy (I got it cheaper)
Baby, pack your van

La la la la la
La la la la la

Old thing now new one
Picking trash is fun
Found it last night right nearby
And it was clear she wouldn't go on
Van door was open, it was drawing near
Wait for morning, it could disappear
Mrs. Spot's eyes were full of fear
Filling up with dread

Deckboards, baby (and they were so near)
Filled the van with them (no reason to buy)
They looked back at empty curbs (her
"brand new" stuff was not far)
She had the ceiling fan (her "brand new"
stuff was not far)
Deckboards, baby (We found it cheaper)

MAILBREAK

To the tune of "Jailbreak" by AC/DC.

There was a time bills were on paper
And now it's a tall tale
Not going to the mailbox
Ending many years of mail

I said, "In my office, I'll be here
I ain't leavin' my home
Ain't going out to the mailbox
I'm staying put and pay from home"

Gonna make a mailbreak
And I'm using home Wi-Fi
Gonna make a mailbreak
Oh, I have no stamps to buy!

All done electronically
All done electronically
And there's no fee

Mailbreak, cables out of here
Mailbreak, no more years.
Mailbreak, wirelessly I can make
Mailbreak, yeah

He said he'd seen people being screwed with
By another plan
They were down, 'cuz bills were late
It's time to take a stand

Cursing started flying everywhere
We're living a bad dream
Shut off notice on the door
With an online address
So payments could be seen

So it was all done electronically
All done electronically
Oh, rid those pesky fees!
Mailbreak.... Mailbreak

I got e-pay now
No more fear

Payments... I'm wifi-ing
Postage... I'm not buying
No checks
A PIN
Info is in

The payments came out
Got an E-receipt right back

Mailbreak
Mailbreak
Mailbreak
Mailbreak
Mailbreak
Mailbreak
Mailbreak
Mailbreak
Mailbreak
Mailbreak

WORK LIKE AN EGYPTIAN

To the tune of "Walk Like an Egyptian" by The Bangles.

You could be walking down the streets
Of Old Egypt owned by pharaohs
Making candlesticks (oh whey oh)
They are baking bread with all this dough

Making things always took a while
But they got done to make a buck
Sold by the Nile (Oh, whey, oh)
There was no need for delivery trucks

Pharaoh lives with many wives say
Whey oh whey oh ay oh whey oh
Work like an Egyptian

They get filthy rich with their pay
They dance around on the sandy floor
They've got the jewels (oh whey oh)
Never enough, they are wanting more

The pharaoh kids will start learning
To be like dad and rule the land
They collect their tax (oh whey oh)
They're working like an Egyptian

Making laws and then declare war
Whey oh whey oh ay oh whey oh
Work like an Egyptian

Finished feat with concrete, take a whack
With your arm, then you take a hack
This is hard, you know (oh whey oh)
In this heat, I'll get a heart attack

They play with rocks in the sand
They're building pyramids with their hands
Hammers and ramps (oh whey oh)
Not like Legos should have a crane

The 2D paintings on the wall
And King Tut's tomb is down the hall
Hieroglyphics show (oh, whey, oh)
The work, the life of Egyptians

In the sand the pyramids still stand
Whey oh whey oh ay oh whey oh
Work like an Egyptian
Work like an Egyptian

GIVIN' A DOG A HOME

To the tune of "Givin' the Dog a Bone" by AC/DC.

She looks at you sadly
Buckling at your weak knees
This is work of the devil
Pant! Pant! It's 90 degrees!

Oh, it's driving me crazy
Till my thinning patience runs dry
Oh, she's needing a bed again
She's needing a bed
Oh, she's needing a bed again

We'll just be givin' a dog a home
Givin' a dog a home
We've just a given a dog a home
Givin' a dog a home
We've just given a dog a home
Givin' a dog a home
We've just given a dog a home
Givin' a dog a home

Oh, was used as a bait dog
Oh, she's lived on the street!
Oh, her ribs had been showing
And sleeping on concrete

Oh, she's needing a bed again
Needing a bed again
She's needing a bed
Needing a bed again
Oh, she's needing a bed again
Needing a bed

We're just givin' a dog a home
Givin' a dog a home
Givin' a dog a home
Givin' a dog a home
We're just givin' a dog a home
Givin' the dog a home
We're just givin' the dog a home
Givin' the dog a home
Let's go!

She got the comfort in our home
Yeah, she even got a big sis
And she likes what we're doing
Yeah, she loves us a lot!
Lovin' everything we got!

Just givin' a dog a home
Givin' a dog a home
Givin' a dog a home
Givin' a dog a home
Givin' a dog a home
Givin' a dog a home

We've just given a dog a home
Givin' a dog a home
Givin' a dog a home
Givin' a dog a home
Givin' a dog a home
Givin' a dog a home
We've just given a dog a home
Givin' a dog a home
We've just given a dog
Givin' a dog
Givin' a dog
We've just given a dog a home

NO RAIN

To the tune of "Cocaine" by Eric Clapton.

If your plant's drooping down
And the grass is real brown... no rain

A blue sky and no clouds
Sun beatin' down... no rain

It's so dry
It's so dry
It's so dry... no rain

Fishing is so rough
And the rafting is tough... no rain

The river is low
With no H_2O... no rain

It's so dry
It's so dry
It's so dry... no rain

No drops in the sky
And all things will just die... no rain

No wet in forecast
Just killing my grass... no rain

It's so dry
It's so dry
It's so dry... no rain

It's so dry
It's so dry
It's so dry... no rain

HAVE NO GRAY MATTER

To the tune of "Nothing Else Matters" by Metallica.

No brain, so empty right here
Couldn't have less between the ears
Forever nothing that I hear
I have no gray matter

Never thinking, I have no brain
Feel nothing, not even my pain
All these words, I cannot say
I have no gray matter

Have no mind so that you can rule
Never did that well in grade school
What kids said was just really cruel
I have no gray matter

I know not what I should do
I know not what I should know
I am slow

No brain, so empty right here
Couldn't have less between the ears
Forever nothing that I hear
I have no gray matter

I know not what I should do
I know not what I should know
I am slow

Never thinking, I have no brain
Feel nothing, not even my pain
All these words, I cannot say
I have no gray matter

Have no mind so that you can rule
Never did that well in grade school
What kids said was just really cruel
I have no gray matter

Always void within my head
All this space is what I dread
I know not what I should do
I know not what I should know
I am slow, yeah, yeah

No brain, so empty right here
Couldn't have less between the ears
Forever nothing that I hear
I have no gray matter

LATE FOR SCHOOL

To the tune of "Sad But True" by Metallica.

Hey (Hey) you awake?
You're the one who hit the snooze
Hey (Hey) you awake?
Bus ride you will lose

They (they) they're at school
You're the only one home now
They (they) they're at school
You are rarely there

Out of bed, sleepy head
Get ready or you will dread
Parental harm until you're dead
Late for school

Out of bed, you're an ass
Get ready, you're late for class
Once again, you'll show up last
You know you're late for school
Late for school

You (You) stayed up late
With your posting and Tik Tok
You (You) stayed up late
You're the one to blame

Do (Do) Do not eat
Don't eat breakfast, there's no time
Do (Do) Do brush teeth
At least get off that grime

Out of bed, sleepy head
Get ready or you will dread
Parental harm until you're dead
Late for school

Out of bed, you' re an ass
Get ready, you're late for class
Once again, you'll show up last
You know you're late for school
Late for school

Out of bed
Get ready
Parental harm

Out of bed (out of bed)
Get ready (Get ready)
Parental harm (parental harm)
You know you're late for school

Hate (Hate) this I hate
This I hate, when you do this
Pay (Pay) Pay the price
Pay in summer school

Hey (Hey) you awake?
You hit the snooze at what cost?
Hey (Hey) you awake?
Bus ride you have lost!

Out of bed, sleepy head
Get ready or you will dread
Parental harm until you're dead
Late for school

Tell me truth, not the lies
Go to school and agonize
I can see it in your eyes

F*** you!
Late for school